EMPRESS WU: BREAKING AND EXPANDING CHINA

Ancient China Books for Kids

Children's Ancient History

BABY PROFESSOR

EDUCATION KIDS

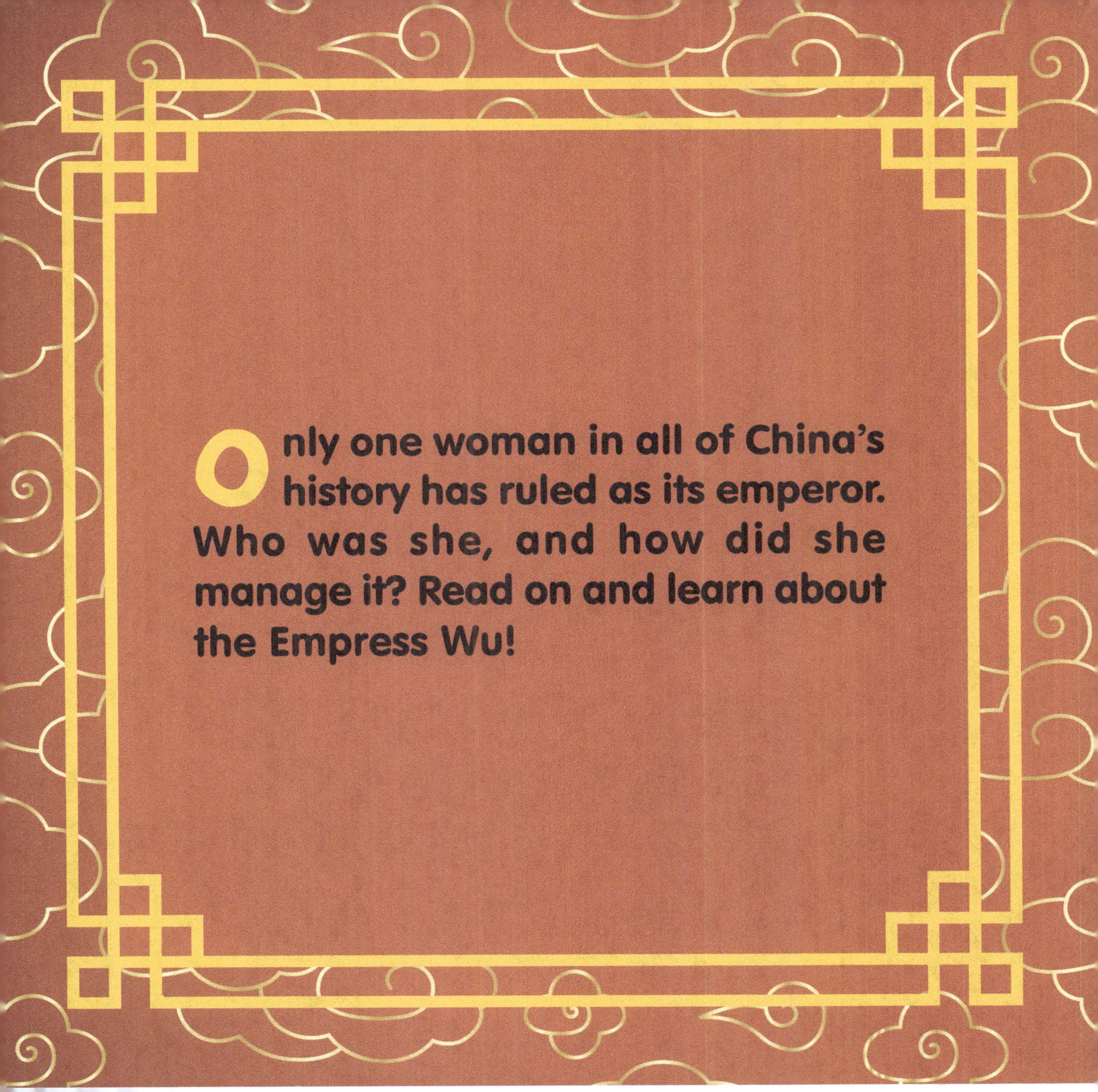

Only one woman in all of China's history has ruled as its emperor. Who was she, and how did she manage it? Read on and learn about the Empress Wu!

CLOSE TO THE THRONE

The Tan dynasty ruled China from 618 to 906 CE. Although men were mostly in charge, it was a time of greater freedom and possibility for women. Several women rose to fame and achieved great things in Chinese culture and politics during this time.

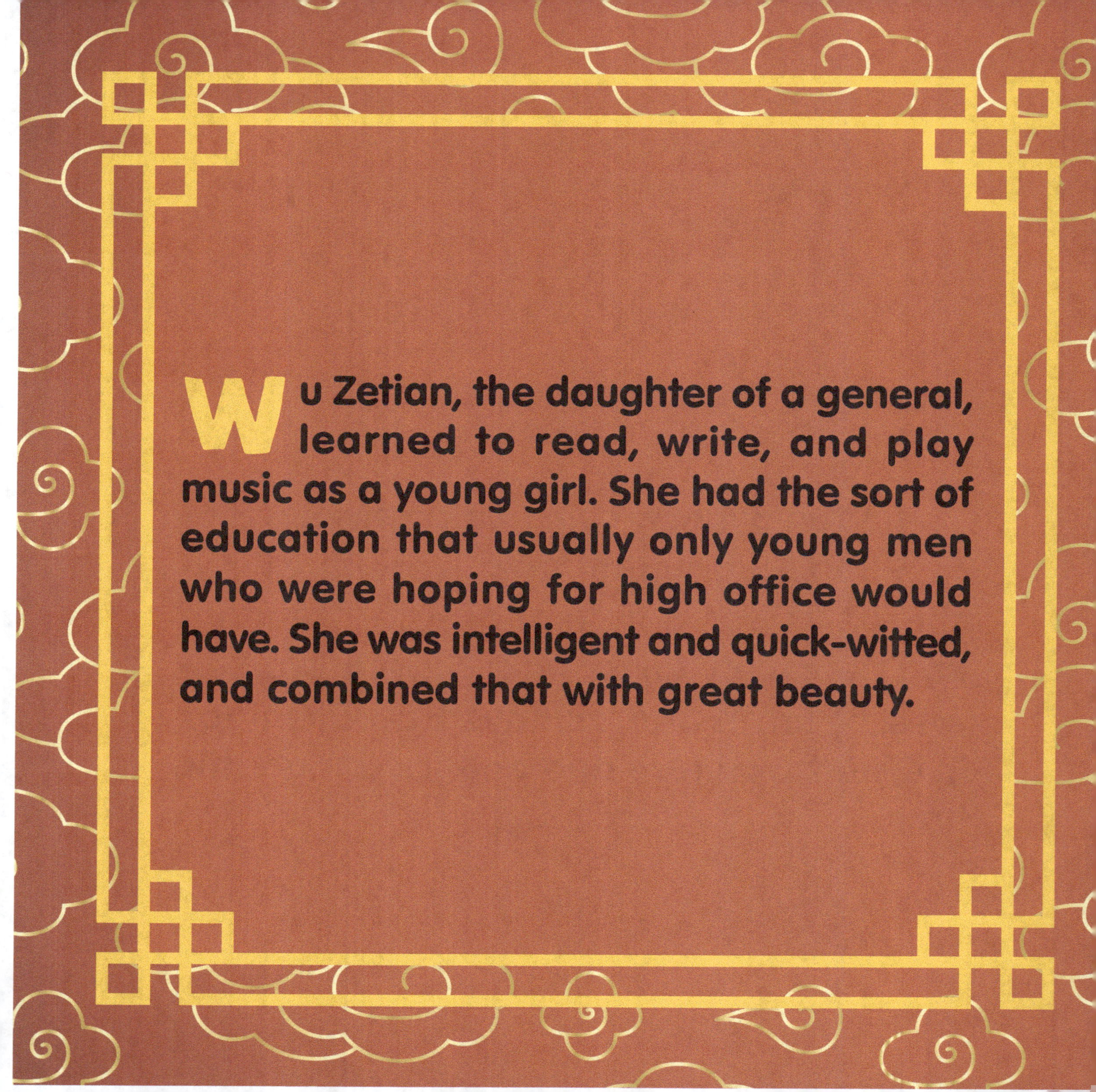

Wu Zetian, the daughter of a general, learned to read, write, and play music as a young girl. She had the sort of education that usually only young men who were hoping for high office would have. She was intelligent and quick-witted, and combined that with great beauty.

WU ZETIAN

TAI TSUNG

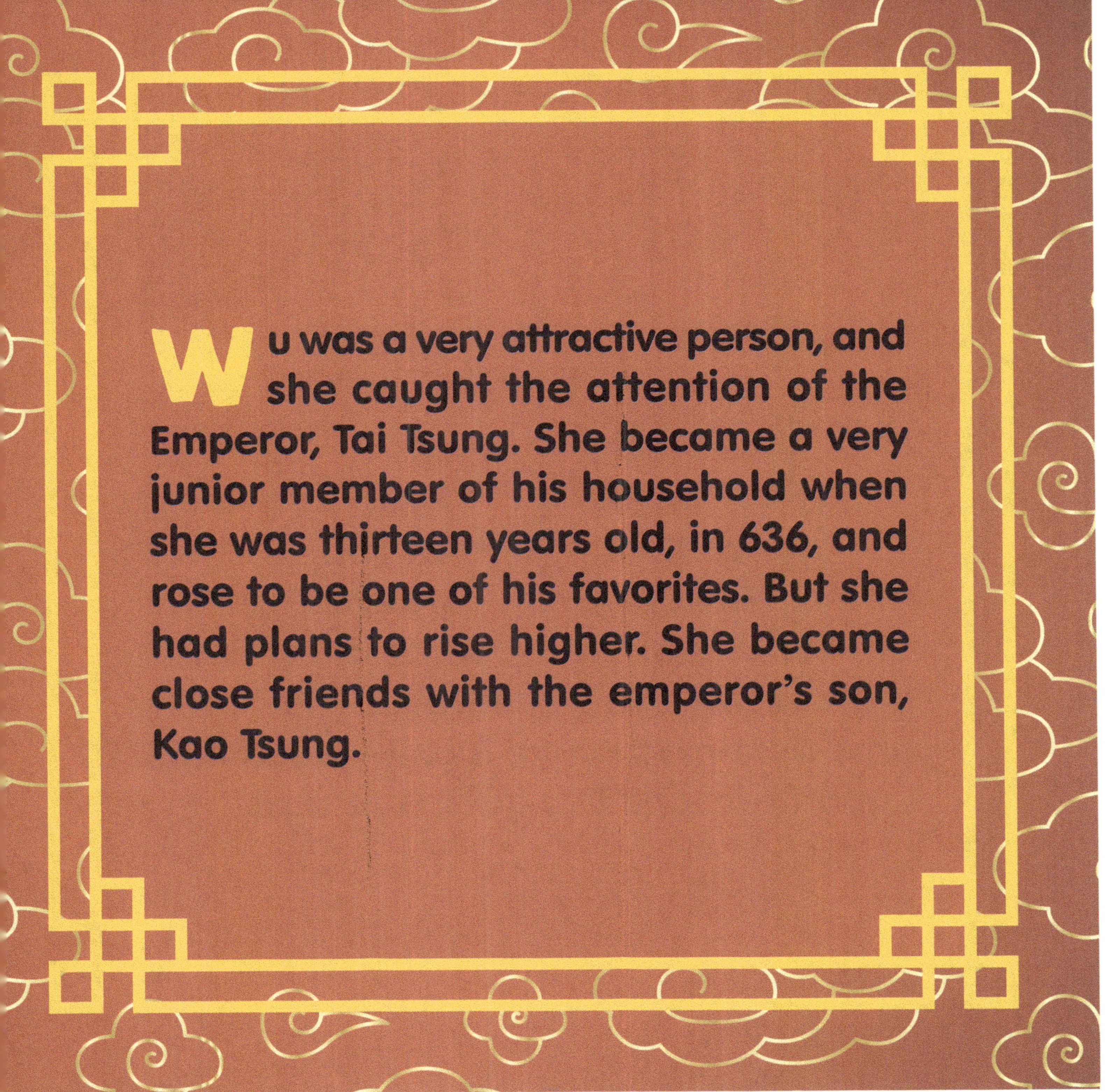

Wu was a very attractive person, and she caught the attention of the Emperor, Tai Tsung. She became a very junior member of his household when she was thirteen years old, in 636, and rose to be one of his favorites. But she had plans to rise higher. She became close friends with the emperor's son, Kao Tsung.

RISING TO POWER

When Tai Tsung died and Kao Tsung became emperor in 650, Wu was about twenty-seven. She was not the official wife of the emperor, but she had had several of his children. In that time, sons were much more highly valued than daughters, and Wu gave him sons.

KAO TSUNG

GIRL HISTORIAN READS A RARE BOOK

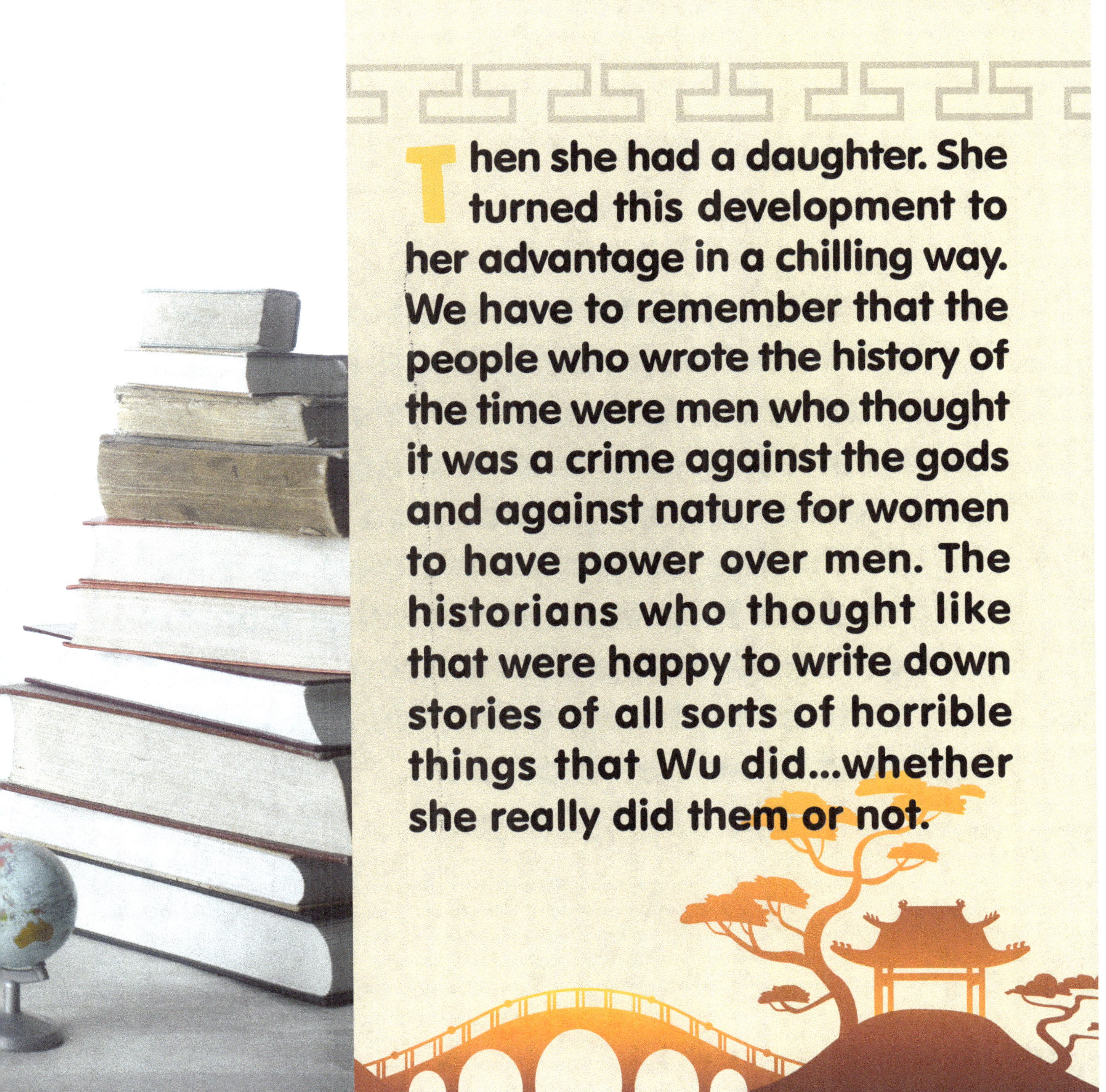

Then she had a daughter. She turned this development to her advantage in a chilling way. We have to remember that the people who wrote the history of the time were men who thought it was a crime against the gods and against nature for women to have power over men. The historians who thought like that were happy to write down stories of all sorts of horrible things that Wu did...whether she really did them or not.

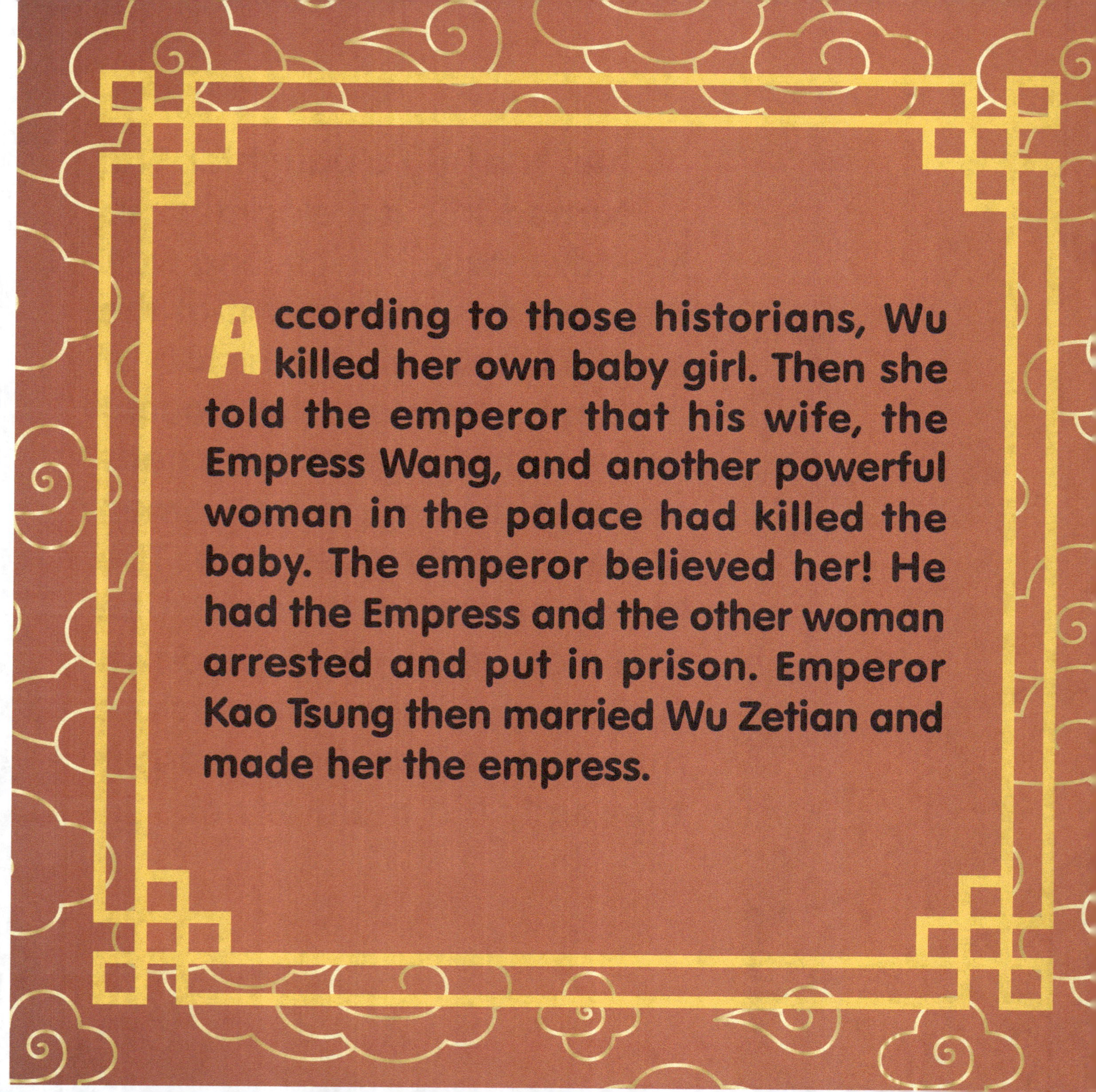

According to those historians, Wu killed her own baby girl. Then she told the emperor that his wife, the Empress Wang, and another powerful woman in the palace had killed the baby. The emperor believed her! He had the Empress and the other woman arrested and put in prison. Emperor Kao Tsung then married Wu Zetian and made her the empress.

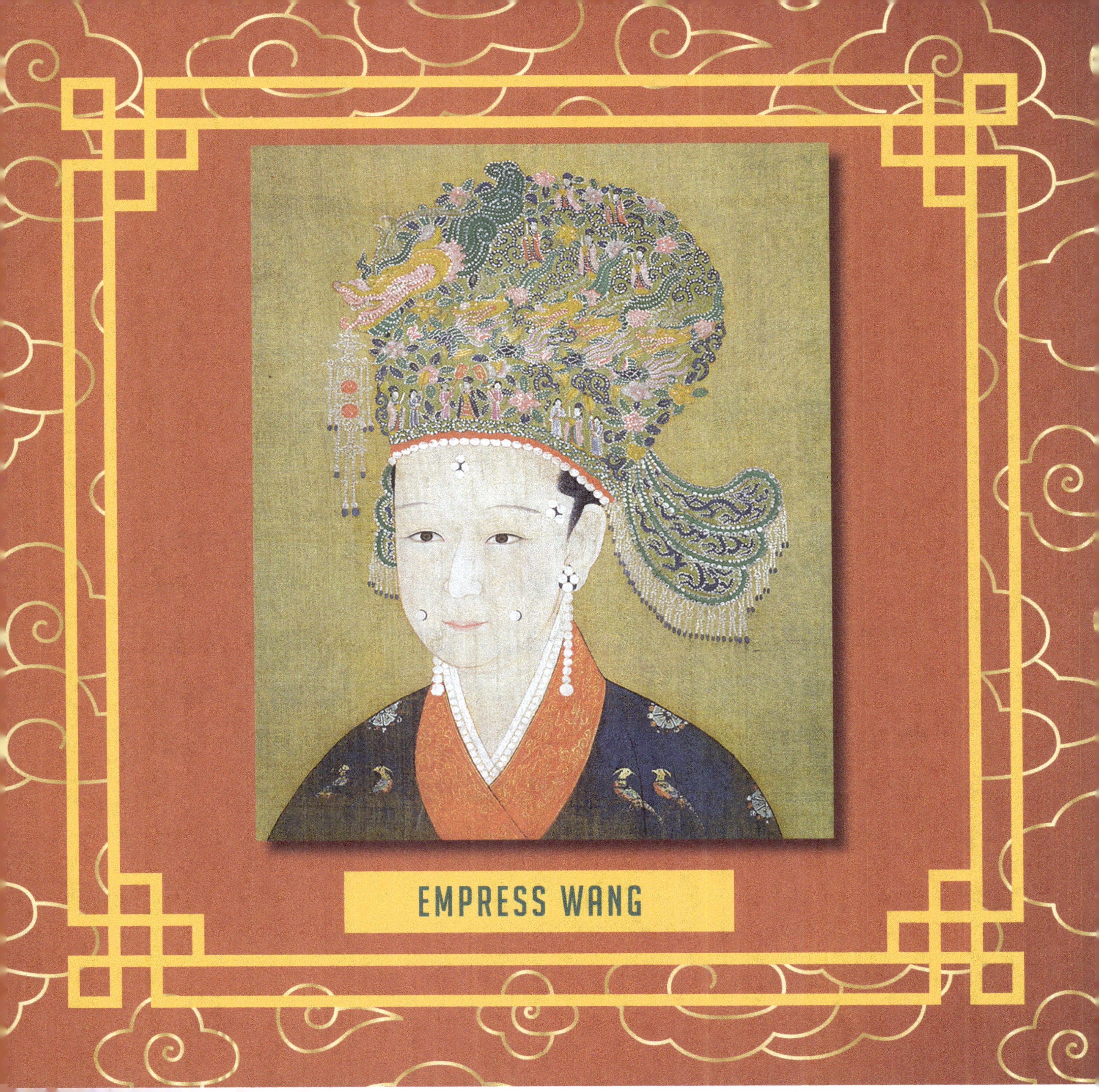

EMPRESS WANG

HOLDING ON TO POWER

Now Wu was the most powerful woman in China, and for five years things were probably as good as she had ever hoped they could be. Then Emperor Kao Tsung had a stroke. He was still alive, but he could not function as emperor.

EMPIRE

He trusted Wu, and she took over the administration of the court. She had a system of spies and secret police who watched and listened for people to do or say things that were disloyal to the emperor—or to the empress. The police would arrest, torture, or even kill those whom Wu saw as potential enemies. During this time the Empress Wang was taken from prison and put to death, probably on Wu's direct orders.

CHINESE KIDS PLAYING

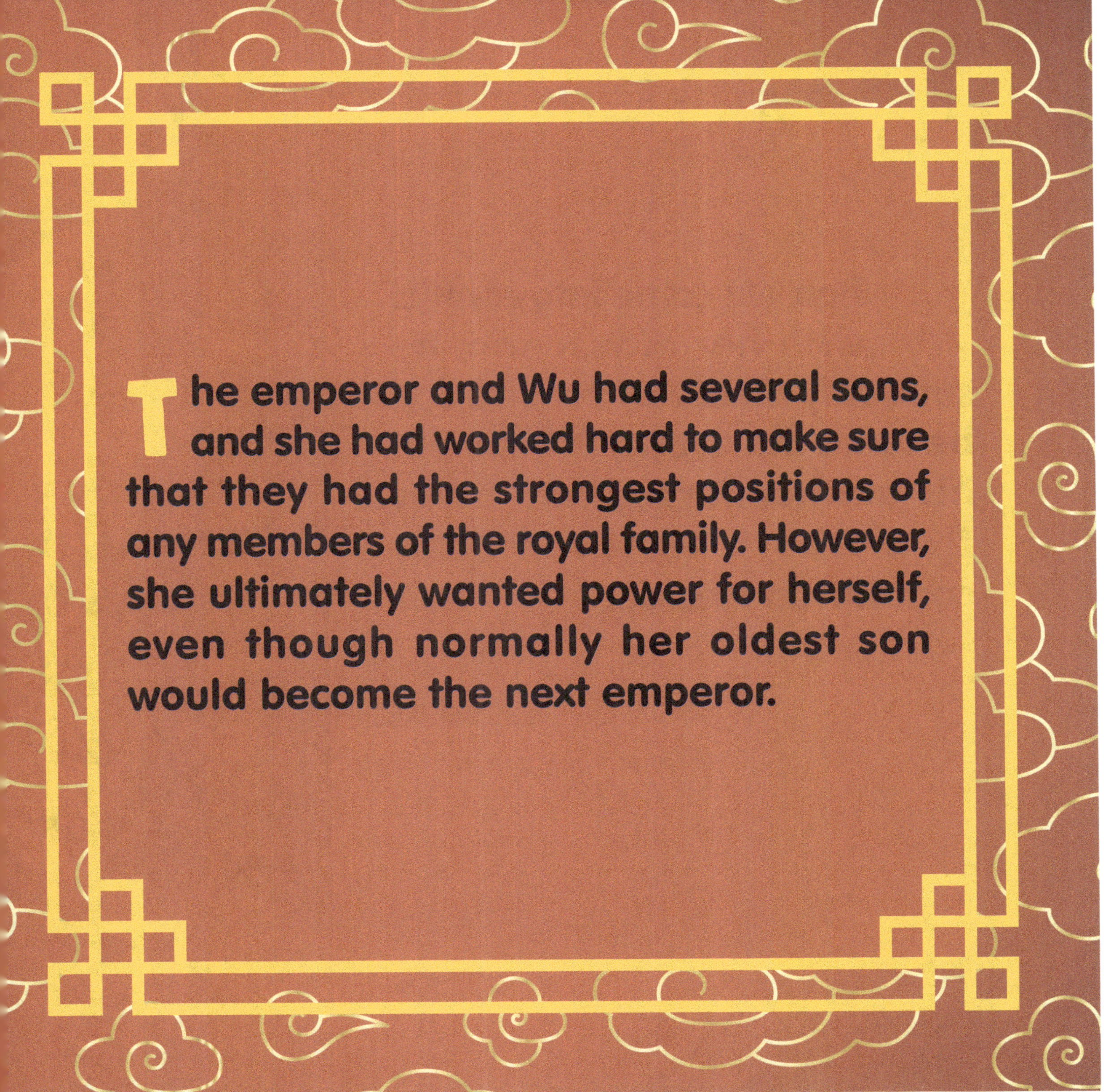

The emperor and Wu had several sons, and she had worked hard to make sure that they had the strongest positions of any members of the royal family. However, she ultimately wanted power for herself, even though normally her oldest son would become the next emperor.

When Wu came into conflict with her eldest son, he suddenly died. Her second son became the Crown Prince, but his mother forced him away from court. He eventually committed suicide.

TOMB OF CROWN PRINCE

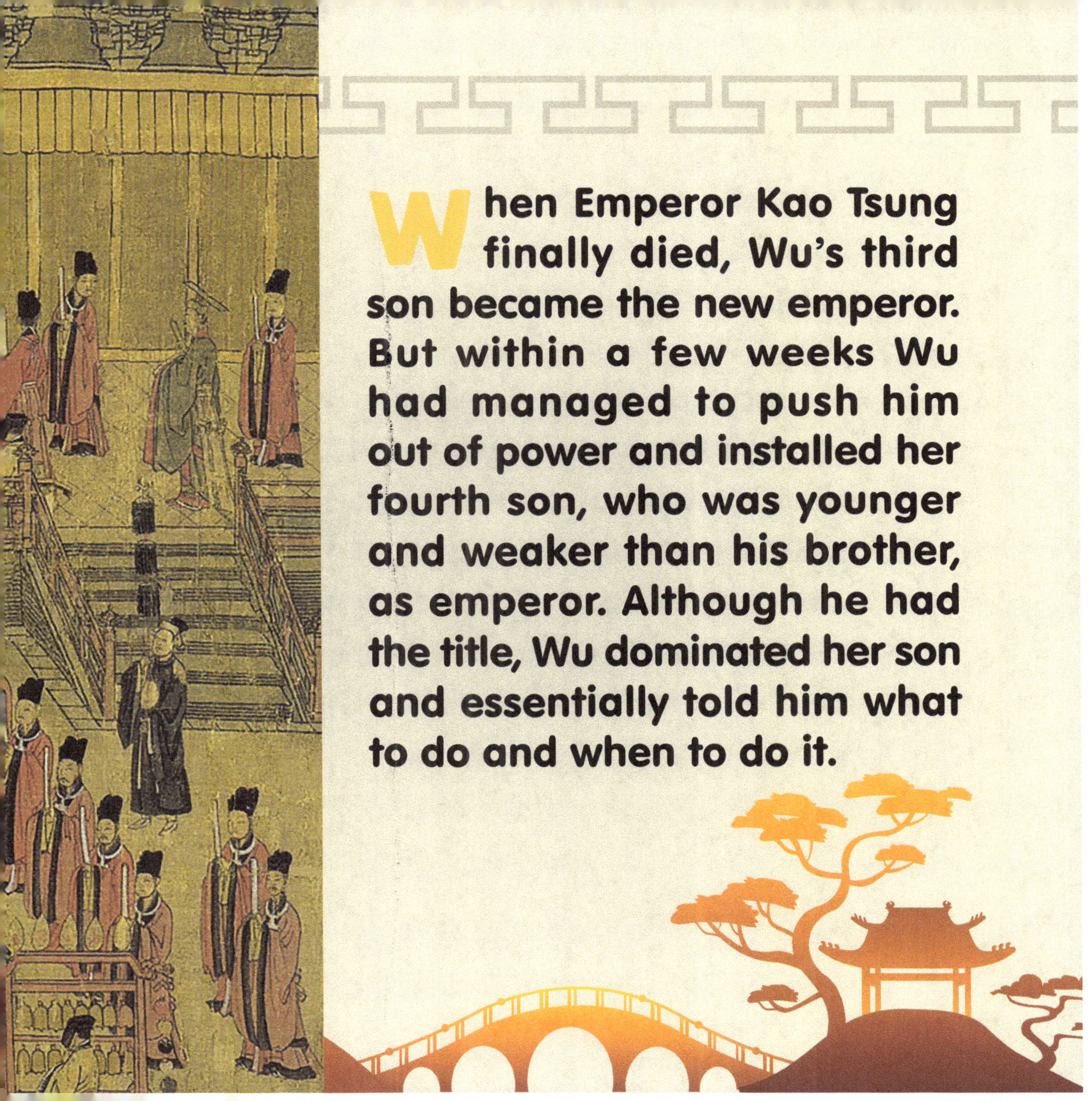

When Emperor Kao Tsung finally died, Wu's third son became the new emperor. But within a few weeks Wu had managed to push him out of power and installed her fourth son, who was younger and weaker than his brother, as emperor. Although he had the title, Wu dominated her son and essentially told him what to do and when to do it.

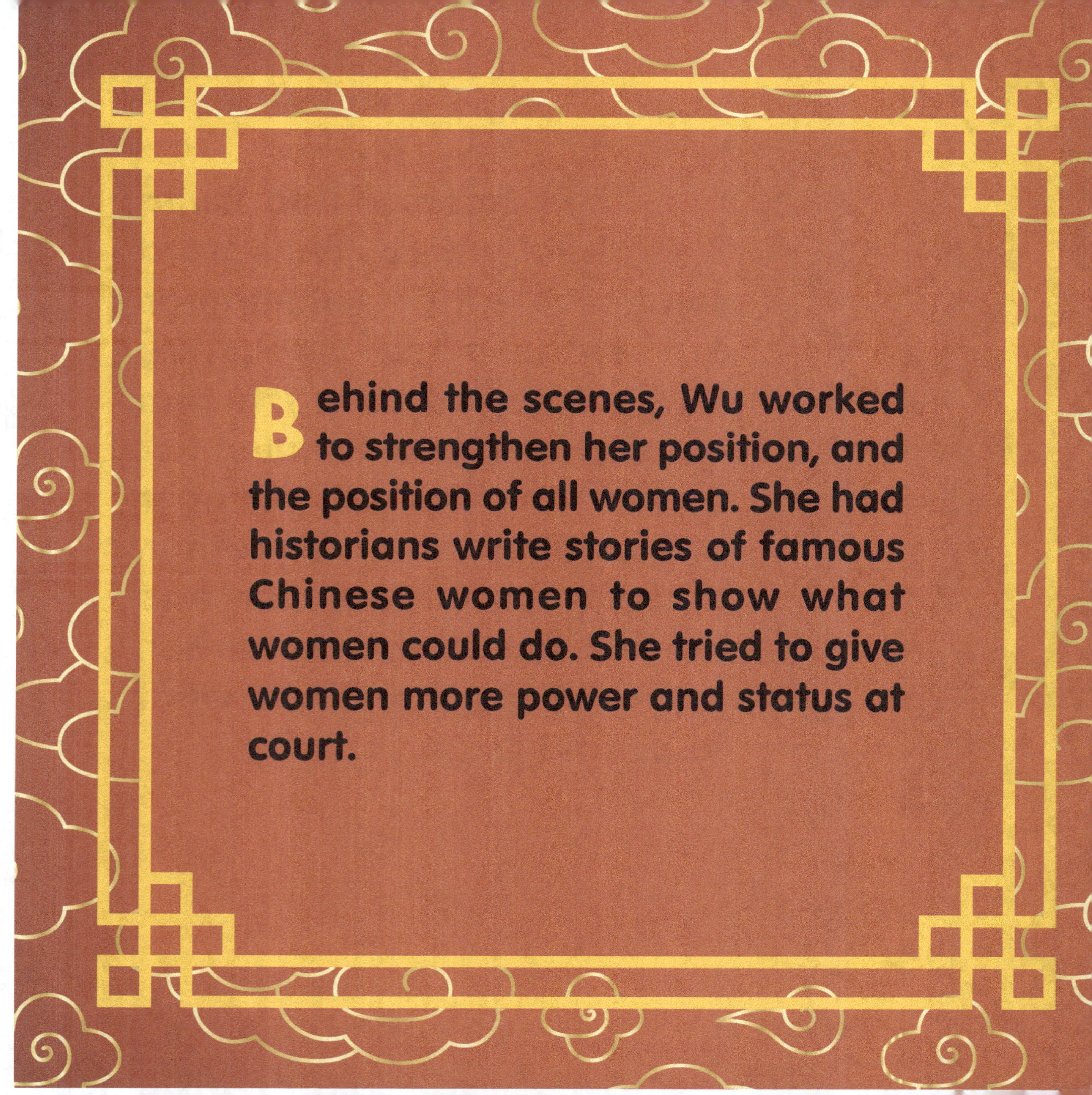

B ehind the scenes, Wu worked to strengthen her position, and the position of all women. She had historians write stories of famous Chinese women to show what women could do. She tried to give women more power and status at court.

COURT LADIES OF THE TANG

PANELS FROM PAGODA, EMPRESS WU

EMPRESS WU

In 690, Wu forced her youngest son to resign as emperor. Wu Zetian was proclaimed the emperor of China. She was now about 64 years old.

If the histories are true, Wu had done many harsh and cruel things to get and hold on to power. However, we should remember that Chinese men had done many similar things when they had a chance to seize power. None of these actions would have been acceptable today, but they were not worse because it was a woman doing them.

TANG PARADISE, CHINA

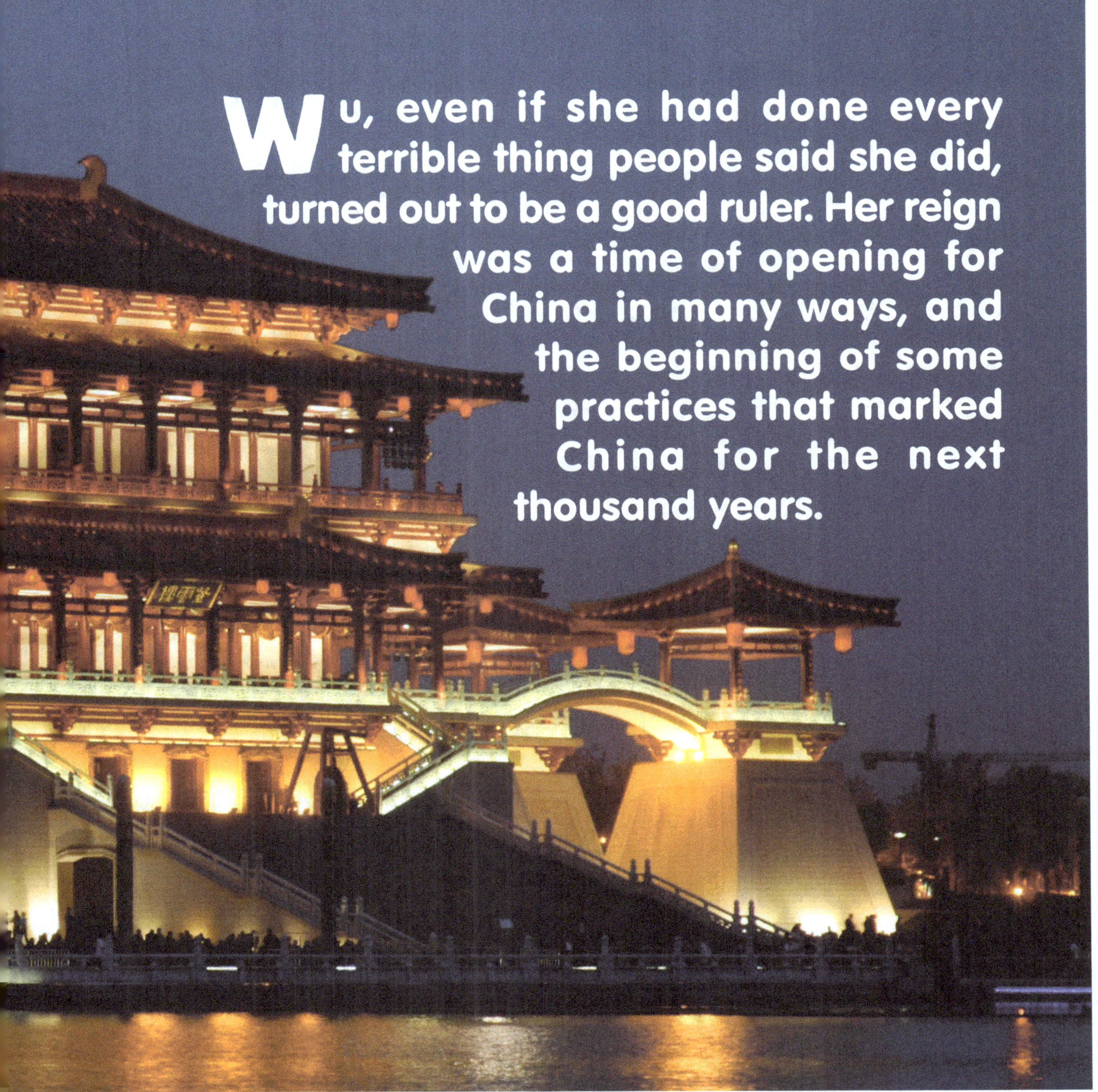

Wu, even if she had done every terrible thing people said she did, turned out to be a good ruler. Her reign was a time of opening for China in many ways, and the beginning of some practices that marked China for the next thousand years.

CHINESE ARMY

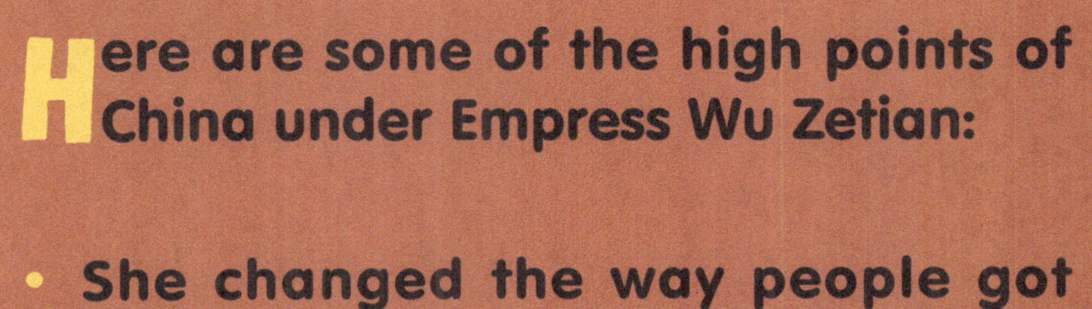

Here are some of the high points of China under Empress Wu Zetian:

- She changed the way people got high office in the government and the army. The traditional way was for the sons of the powerful, or well-connected people, to get high office. Now, under the Empress Wu, people had to demonstrate that they had the skill and knowledge for the job they wanted, by taking exams. This started to move China away from government by the nobility and toward government by scholars.

She reduced taxes on the peasants
and invested in canals, roads, and
other public works to improve crop
production and to make it easier to
get food and other goods from the
country to the cities.

WINDING ROAD OF TIANMEN MOUNTAIN

She rewarded good administrators and punished those who were incompetent, cruel, or corrupt. Both food production and the quality of life of the peasants improved dramatically.

OILSEED FIELD

- She supported Buddhism, the study of the teachings of Buddha, over the traditional Chinese religion, Daoism. She invited important Buddhist scholars, teachers and artists to China (Buddhism developed in India), and supported building great Buddhist temples. Under the Empress Wu, Buddhism became the strongest religion and philosophical path in China.

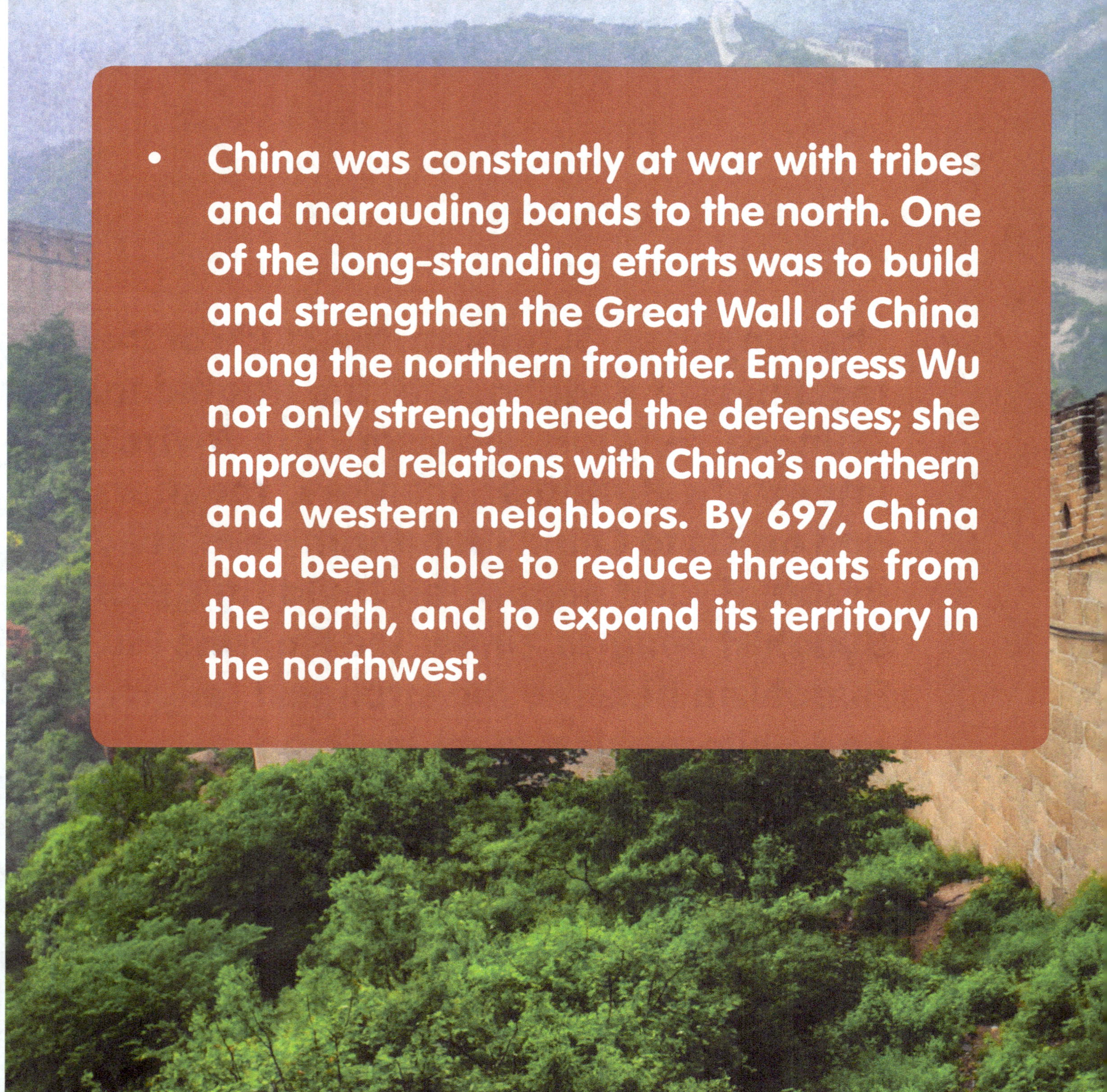

China was constantly at war with tribes and marauding bands to the north. One of the long-standing efforts was to build and strengthen the Great Wall of China along the northern frontier. Empress Wu not only strengthened the defenses; she improved relations with China's northern and western neighbors. By 697, China had been able to reduce threats from the north, and to expand its territory in the northwest.

THE GREAT WALL OF CHINA

• Empress Wu was not afraid of war, though. During her reign, China sent armies into what is now North Korea, conquering that area and adding it to China.

- She had manuals of farming techniques printed and widely distributed. This not only helped improve the harvests, but it also stimulated Chinese literature and the idea that printed material should be widely available. She even introduced about thirty new characters into Chinese writing.

CHINESE ANTIQUE CALLIGRAPHY

SILK TRADING ROUTE BETWEEN CHINA AND INDIA

- The Silk Road is a series of routes between China and the Middle East that for thousands of years has been a main way of carrying goods between China and the rest of the world. This route had been closed for years because of a plague epidemic to the west, and fears that traders would bring the plague to China. Under Empress Wu, the Silk Road was able to reopen.

DECLINE AND DEATH

E mpress Wu presided over an era when China was prosperous and largely at peace. There were few threats from outside the country, and little unrest within China. Over time, she reduced her use of her secret police force and fewer people ended up being imprisoned for real or imagined crimes.

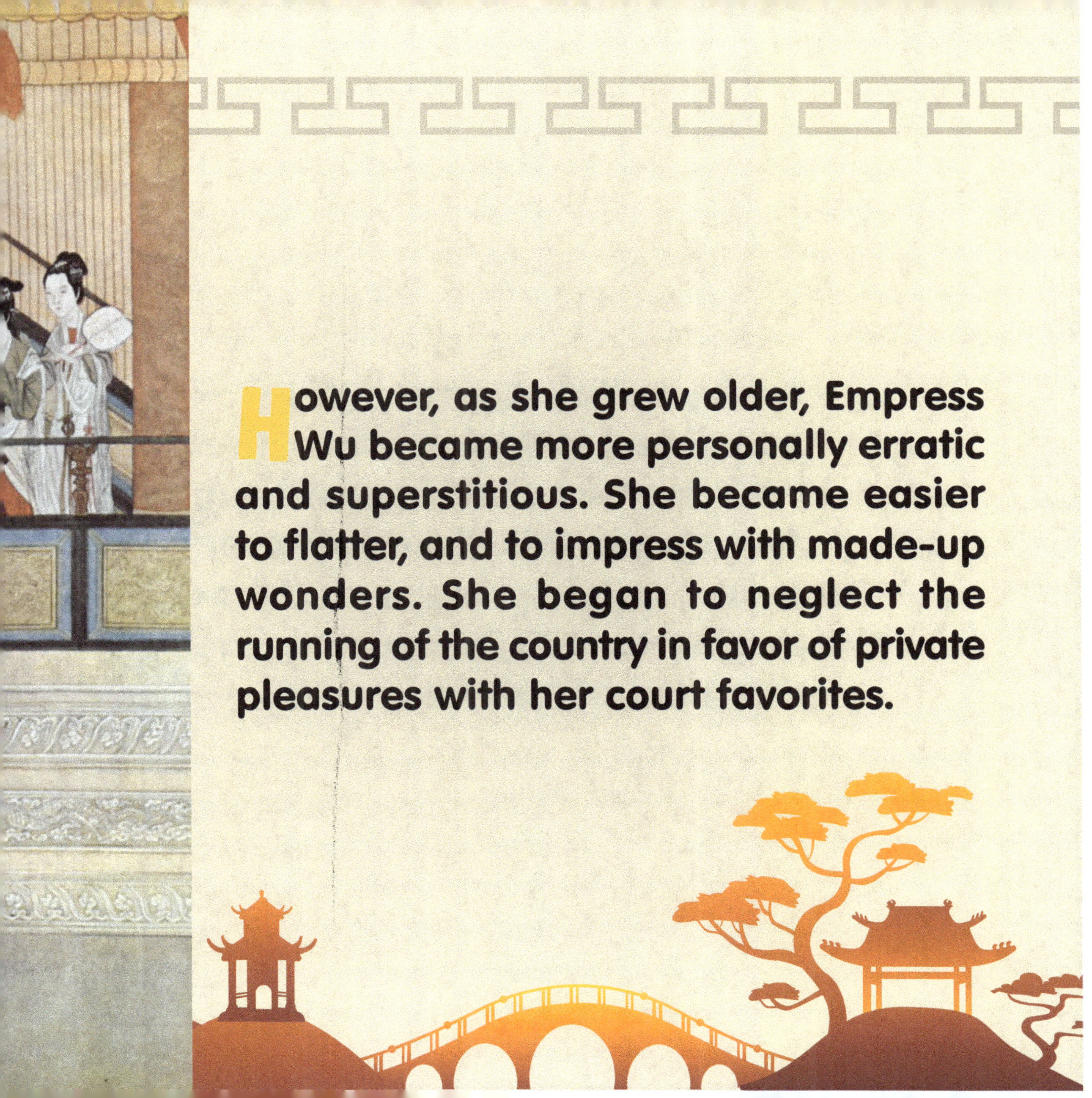

However, as she grew older, Empress Wu became more personally erratic and superstitious. She became easier to flatter, and to impress with made-up wonders. She began to neglect the running of the country in favor of private pleasures with her court favorites.

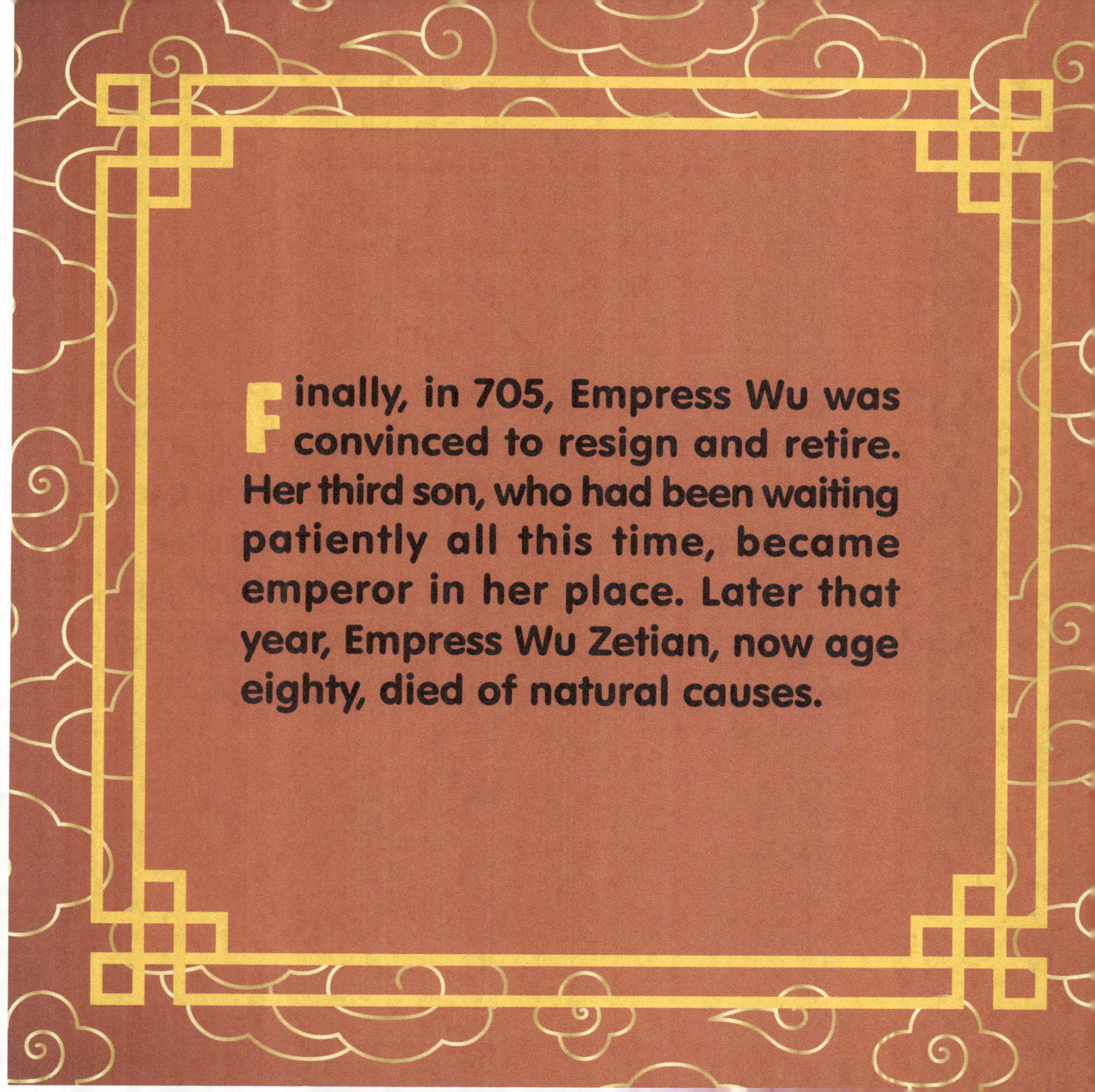

inally, in 705, Empress Wu was convinced to resign and retire. Her third son, who had been waiting patiently all this time, became emperor in her place. Later that year, Empress Wu Zetian, now age eighty, died of natural causes.

EMPRESS WU STONE SLAB

The custom in China at the time was to put up a huge stone slab in front of the emperor's tomb. The slab was blank until the emperor died. Then historians would write all the great things of the emperor's reign on the slab. Reflecting the disapproval many still felt about having a woman in charge, even if her reign was successful, the slab in front of Wu Zetian's tomb remained blank: nobody wrote her history.

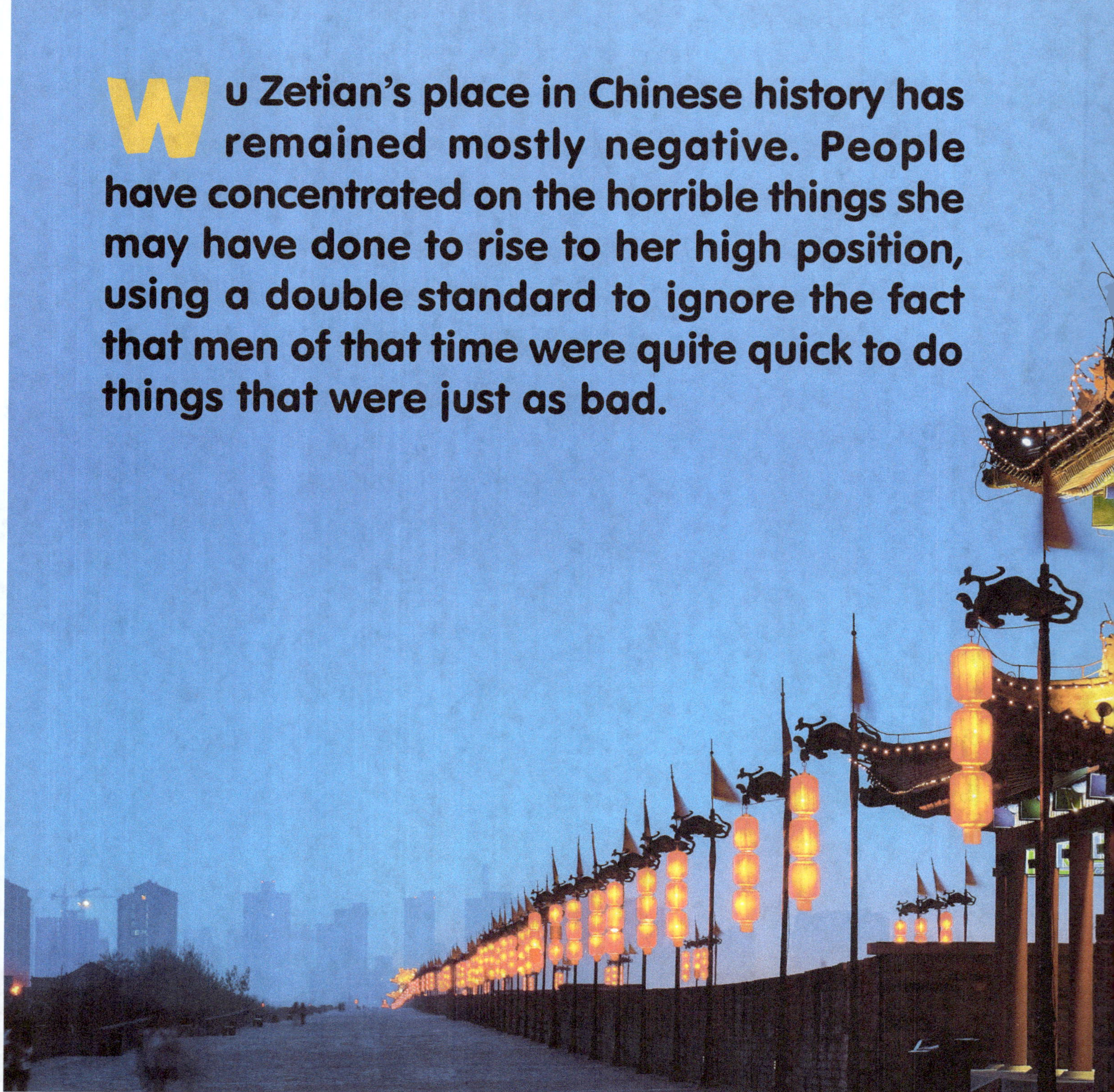

Wu Zetian's place in Chinese history has remained mostly negative. People have concentrated on the horrible things she may have done to rise to her high position, using a double standard to ignore the fact that men of that time were quite quick to do things that were just as bad.

A GREAT EMPIRE

The Chinese culture has existed for thousands of years. Learn more about its high points in Baby Professor books like Who Built the Great Wall of China?, Trade and Commerce in Ancient China, How did Your Chinese Ancestors Live?, and The Chinese Festivals.

Visit

BABY PROFESSOR
EDUCATION KIDS

www.BabyProfessorBooks.com

to download Free Baby Professor eBooks
and view our catalog of new and exciting
Children's Books